Imprint / Impressum
Michael Scheidl
scheidl.publishing@gmail.com
Hauptstraße 13/9
2564 Weissenbach
AUSTRIA

Made in the USA
Monee, IL
07 July 2022

99254988R00072